CELEBRATION

Hanukkah

WOMEN'S LEAGUE FOR
CONSERVATIVE JUDAISM

Front Cover: *Ḥanukkah Lamp*
Frankfurt-am-Main, circa 1750-60.
The Jewish Museum, under the
auspices of the Jewish Theological
Seminary of America.

All artwork from The Jewish Museum collection
courtesy of Art Resource, New York, NY.

First Edition November 1990
ISBN # 0-936293-02-0

© Women's League for Conservative Judaism
   48 East 74 Street
   New York, New York 10021

Introduction

*". . .She'asah nissim la'avotaynu ba'yamim
ha'hem baz'man hazeh."*

*". . .Who performed wonders for our ancestors
in every generation."*

*F*rom generation to generation, the Ḥanukkah celebration has been a vibrant part of Jewish life, observed in the home by young and old. Change manifests itself in every generation and today, we build our contemporary Ḥanukkah celebrations on traditional experiences blended with our own cultural nuances.

Whether the festival of Ḥanukkah relies upon a historic source or seasonal lore, it is evident that the *mitzvah* of kindling the Ḥanukkah lights "is an exceedingly precious

*Lion of Judah Dreidel by Arie Salomon and Shirley Kagan, solid brass,
limited edition, 1990. In The Spirit Studio, New York.*

one, and one should be particularly careful to fulfill it," according to Maimonides.

In this Women's League for Conservative Judaism Celebration Manual, you will find an overview of the historical background and observance of Ḥanukkah. It is followed by specific ideas for celebration: games, crafts, decorations, music, and recipes. The book ends with suggestions for study, including some challenging discussion questions and a comprehensive list of resource materials.

It is a meaningful educational tool for groups, families and individuals. We hope you will use this Manual to create your very own Ḥanukkah celebration. To enhance its observance year after year, we have provided blank pages for your personal notes.

The Reading and Editorial Committee expresses appreciation to Women's League President Evelyn Auerbach for all her warmth and encouragement in creating the Celebration Series. We wish to acknowledge the contributions of the many dedicated volunteers who helped to research, organize and write this Manual: Hadassah Blocker, Janet Goldberg, Sylvia Levin, Blanche Meisel, Deborah Miller, Marion Mohl, Janis Popp and Lora Lee Spiro.

Our special thanks to Women's League Vice President Elaine Ravich, who served as

Coordinator of the project. We also acknowledge the valuable guidance of the Women's League professional staff: Maureen Wise, Public Relations Director; Edya Arzt, Education Director; and Bernice Balter, Executive Director.

Helene Schachter, Chairman
Reading and Editorial Committee

The History of Ḥanukkah

The holiday of Ḥanukkah holds a special place in the hearts and minds of Jewish people everywhere. Rich in historic significance, Ḥanukkah is eagerly celebrated each year in Jewish homes throughout the world by young and old alike.

Tree of Knowledge M'norah — cast brass, Eastern Europe, 19th century. Gift of Dr. Harry G. Friedman. The Jewish Museum, New York.

Like Passover, Ḥanukkah is commemorated as a festival of freedom. In Egypt, Moses led the enslaved Hebrews in an uprising which marked the beginning of a significant era for Israel as a people. In Judea, 1000 years later, the Hasmonean priest, Mattathias, and his five sons led a small band of dedicated Jews who routed the armies of Antiochus Epiphanes, King of Syria.

Unlike other Jewish festivals, we know the origin and exact date of Ḥanukkah. The story of this unique struggle is recorded in *Maccabees I and II*, two of the many books of the *Apocrypha*, the collection of non-canonical semi-sacred literature. The story is told in the *Scroll of Antiochus*, a brief work probably produced in Babylon. From both of these sources we learn that the Maccabean uprising in 167 B.C.E. was precipitated by the decrees of King Antiochus. He hoped to eradicate the religious and cultural separatism of the Jews, which threatened his monolithic Hellenized empire.

From the time of the Babylonian exile in the fifth century B.C.E. to the revolt of the Maccabees, Jews lived peacefully, freely practicing and developing a spiritual life based on the Torah and centered about the Temple. When Alexander the Great conquered the Near East, many Jews fell under the spell of Greek culture and voluntarily assimilated. Upon Alexander's death his empire was divided: the Ptolemies ruled Egypt; the Seleucids controlled Syria. Palestine was caught in the middle, as the two rival factions waged an ongoing war.

When Antiochus IV ascended the Syrian throne, he sought to secure his position against the threat of Egypt and Rome by Hellenizing the diverse nationalities of his kingdom. This aroused the resentment of the devoutly religious elements of the population. They recognized that surrender to Greek culture would signal a defeat for Judaism, for Hellenism emphasized indulgence in physical pleasures, the abandonment of moral restraints and the acceptance of paganism and idol-worship.

Antiochus ordered the Jews to cease worshipping in the Temple; to profane the Sabbath and the festivals; to build altars and shrines to Greek idols; to eat the meat of swine; to stop circumcizing their sons. To disobey any of these prohibitions meant instant death. The horrors steadily mounted as the Temple Sanctuary was desecrated and a gigantic statue of Zeus was raised on a pedestal behind the altar. The Temple Courts, formerly the site of the beautiful songs of the Levites, became the scene of revelry and idol worship.

Although the High Priest, Jason, and many Jewish aristocrats collaborated in paying homage to the Greek gods, the pious Jews refused to acquiesce. Thousands died rather than obey the decrees of Antiochus; thousands more fled into the wilderness. Their strong belief in Judaism led to a course of action which marked the revival of nationalist sentiments and the tradition of *Kiddush HaShem*—martyrdom for the sanctification of God. These rebels were the first martyrs in history to struggle for freedom of conscience.

The uprising in 167 B.C.E. was the inevitable result of these events. In the village of Modi'in, an aged Hasmonian priest, Mattathias, ignited the spark of revolt. When a Jewish apostate made a sacrifice to the Greek gods in the town square, the enraged priest slew the traitor. Turning to the crowd, he cried, "Who is for the Lord, follow me!" Together with several hundred followers, he and his five sons fled into the

Judean hills. Judah, the middle son (who was called Maccabee — the Hammer), soon emerged as the strategist who led the brilliant attacks against the superior forces of the Syrian army. The cry of Judah and his guerrilla band became: *"Mi khamokha ba'aylim Adonai"*—thus the acronym by which they became known—MACCABEE. The stories of their heroic deeds and miraculous triumphs over the well-armed and superbly trained troops of Antiochus remain incredible. Their decisive victory in 165 B.C.E. marked an important milestone: for the first time in the annals of history, a war for religious freedom was fought and won.

Re-entering the Holy City of Jerusalem, the victorious insurgents found the Temple profaned, its great gates burned and its courts filled with idols. The angry victors smashed the statues, cleared the courts and purified the Sanctuary.

On the twenty-fifth day of Kislev, the Temple was rededicated. The great M'norah was rekindled. The Congregation of Israel rejoiced for eight days, decreeing that on this same day each year Jews were to commemorate the rededication of the Temple with an eight day celebration, to be known as Ḥanukkah.

Ḥanukkah Lamp silver, Frankfurt am Main, c. 1680. The Jewish Museum, New York.

Rabbis of the Mishnah and Talmud did not want to commemorate a war, although it was fought for religious freedom. Some commentaries hold that the "small miracle" with which we are all familiar—that of the one cruse of oil which burned for eight days—was actually a signal from God that the victory in the war did indeed merit commemoration. Others maintain that such a miracle never occurred and the Rabbis of the period sanctioned the holiday of Ḥanukkah nevertheless. It was not until centuries later, when the Talmud was compiled, that this legend was used to justify the commemoration of a war. We find the following explanation in *Bameh Madlikin* in the Talmud: "When the Hasmoneans prevailed against the Greeks, they searched the Temple and found only one jar of oil, which stood untouched and undefiled, with the seal of the High Priest. It contained sufficient oil for one day's lighting. But a miracle was wrought therein and they lit the lamps with it for eight days." A contrived account or an actual miracle? We shall never know, but the story of the oil burning for eight days has captured the hearts of those who enjoy the magical and the miraculous.

For many Jews there is another interpretation. The epic of Ḥanukkah celebrates the following concept: there exists no power on earth able to crush the free, aspiring spirit in men. This triumphant view was expressed by the Prophet Z'khar'yah three and a half centuries before the Maccabbean revolt: "Not by might nor by power, but by My Spirit, said the Lord of

Hosts." (*Z'khar'yah* 4:6) Because of its inspired message, this chapter was chosen as the Haftarah of the first Sabbath of Ḥanukkah. We light the M'norah to recall that the faithful Jews, in defiance of the decrees of Antiochus, did not allow "the light of Torah" to be extinguished.

The festival of Ḥanukkah has achieved great importance in modern Jewish life, observed by Jews today as one of the most meaningful Jewish holidays.

Stone Ḥanukkah Lamp — roughly hewn slab, Palestine, early Tannaitic period. Temple Israel of Great Neck, New York.

Observance in Synagogue and Home

Masada Hanukkah Lamp by Moshe Zabari, silver, New York, 1967. Collection of Mr. and Mrs. Stanley D. Ferst; on loan to The National Museum of American Jewish History, Philadelphia.

How does a festival take shape and form and substance? Ḥanukkah is not of biblical origin, but was decreed after a military victory in 165 B.C.E. Although many once important festivals have long been forgotten, Ḥanukkah has endured. Perhaps the appeal of the holiday lies in its universal theme of freedom, the inspiring message of its legends, and the warmth of its traditions.

The first celebrations took place in the Second Temple, where the festival of "dedication" (Ḥanukkah) mirrored the image of the Festival of Tabernacles (Sukkot). The lulav was waved; Psalm 30 ("Mizmor Shir Ḥanukkat HaBa'yit"— "A psalm, a song for Ḥanukkah") was sung by the Levites; torches and lamps were kindled, giving rise to Ḥanukkah's other descriptive title, "Ḥag Ha'Urim" ("The Festival of Lights").

It is by this name, the "festival of lights", that Josephus refers to the celebration, which in his time (approximately 79 C.E.) had spread beyond Jerusalem. By the second half of the first century C.E., the Rabbis had established the custom of kindling the Ḥanukkah lights. (Our rabbis have taught: "The mitzvah of Ḥanukkah mandates that a lamp be lit for every man and his household. The zealous provide a lamp for each member of the household . . ." and "Women are also obliged to kindle the Ḥanukkah lamp since they were also included in the miracle." Shabbat 21b) These Talmudic rulings effectively made Ḥanukkah a family holiday as its customs spread throughout ancient Israel.

Ḥanukkah is rich in tradition. The addition of a ninth candle, the Shamash (servant), with which the other lights are kindled, is based on two Rabbinic injunctions: we are not to kindle one Ḥanukkah light with another, nor may we use the Ḥanukkah lights for illumination. Many customs observed years ago remain in practice today. In Jewish homes, candles are lit and *ḥanukkiot* are placed near windows for all to see. Families join in special holiday games and songs, gifts are exchanged and children receive Ḥanukkah *gelt*. Foods prepared in oil, such as latkes and jelly doughnuts, are eaten. Among the Sephardim, feasts for the children with special competitions are arranged.

In modern day Israel, Ḥanukkah represents the continuation of the struggle for Jewish nationhood, Jewish identity and Jewish independence. Large *ḥanukkiot* are placed atop water towers in every village. In the cities, huge *ḥanukkiot*, visible for great distances, are displayed at synagogues, schools, the Knesset and other public buildings. An exciting torchlight relay race starting at Modi'in adds to the festive spirit.

Ḥanukkah Lamp cast brass, Polish or Russian, 1753. Gift of Dr. Harry G. Friedman, The Jewish Museum, New York.

Observance in the Synagogue

In synagogues, Ḥanukkah lights are kindled each day following afternoon *Minḥah* services. The *"Al Hanissim"* prayer, describing the victory of the Maccabees, is added when reciting the *Amidah*. The complete *Hallel* service praising God for miracles is recited. The Torah is read each morning, with the readings for the eight days taken successively from *B'midbar* 7. This chapter deals with the gifts of the twelve princes of Israel on the occasion of the dedication of the Tabernacle altar in the wilderness. On the eighth day, *Numbers* 7:54-89 is read, the last four verses referring to the kindling of the lights of the holy *m'norot* (candlesticks).

At least one Shabbat always falls on Ḥanukkah. The Haftarah for that Sabbath is *Z'khar'yah* 2:14—4:7, which contains the well-known verse, "Not by might, nor by power, but by My Spirit . . ." When Ḥanukkah encompasses two Sabbaths, *M'lakhim Alef* 7:40-50, a description of the furnishings of the Temple, is read.

Travelling Ḥanukkah Lamp Handwrought and chased silver, Poland, c. 1900. Temple Israel of Great Neck, New York.

Children of the World M'norah by Carol Brull, ceramic, Georgia, 1990. Galerie Robin, Nashville.

Observance in the Home

Beginning on the eve of the 25th of Kislev and continuing for eight days, the *ḥanukkiah* is lit every evening any time after sunset. After kindling the lights Ashkenazim traditionally sing *Maoz Tzur.* The popular verses were written in the thirteenth century by a man named Mordecai, who wrote it in the form of an acrostic, with the first letter of each line spelling out his name. The melody that we sing today is a combination of a sixteenth century German church hymn and a folk melody. While the Sephardim often recite *Psalm 30* at home, the

Ashkenazim rarely do—although some may recite it in the synagogue. During Ḥanukkah, the *"Al Hanissim"* prayer is added to the *Birkat HaMazon.*

It is customary that the woman of the house does no work while the candles are burning. For her, the holiday becomes more unique, as other family members prepare and serve the evening meal.

Ḥanukkah is known for its lively games, the most famous of which is *"dreidel".* Dreidel, or *"trendel"* (from the German *"drehen"*) was a popular game in Germany, Austria and Poland. Tradition holds that Jews, forbidden to study Torah during the Greek occupation of Israel, used their *dreidels* to study secretly. To keep from being discovered by Greek officials, the Jews would take out their *dreidels* and pretend to be playing games. Enjoyed for centuries, the *dreidel (s'vivon* in Hebrew) certainly has an intriguing history.

The Ḥanukkah lamp, which is called a *ḥanukkiah* or *m'norah,* has also evolved through the ages. The nine branched candelabrum that we light today has developed from the seven branched *m'norah,* designed by the biblical artisan Bezalel according to God's specifications, as conveyed by Moses. We read in *Exodus* that he fashioned the seven branches of his *m'norah* to symbolize the seven days of creation. His design closely resembles the salvia plant, which grows abundantly throughout Israel and is known today as the Jerusalem Moriah. Moses decreed that Bezalel's golden *m'norah* was to be placed in the Tabernacle which the Israelites carried with them as they wandered through the wilderness of the Sinai Desert. King Solomon's First Temple (1000-586 B.C.E.) was illuminated by ten gold *m'norot;* the Second Temple (520 B.C.E.-70 A.D.) was lit by one.

The nine branched *m'norot* that we use to commemorate Ḥanukkah were originally simple clay Greco-Roman lamps. Later *ḥanukkiot* were mounted on elongated vertical bases. Talmudic law held that the lamps were to be placed outside the entrances to homes in order to proclaim the Ḥanukkah miracle. (Our Rabbis taught: "It is incumbent to place the Ḥanukkah lamp by the door of one's house. . . if one dwells in an upper chamber, he places it at the window near the street. But in times of danger it is (acceptable) to place it on the table." *Shabbat* 21b)

The Middle Ages saw the development of metal *ḥanukkiot,* which were able to be hung on the walls. By the sixteenth century, Spanish Jewish refugees had introduced the back-walled *ḥanukkiah* to Eastern Europe. During the Renaissance in Italy, *ḥanukkiot* were elaborately decorated. At that time, German Jews began to use an eight branched standing *ḥanukkiah,* especially in the synagogues. Polish Jews added legs as it was their custom to place the lamp on a windowsill or table. In Iraq and Persia, the Jews continued the ancient custom of round *ḥanukkiot* made of stone or metal dating from the period of the Babylonian Talmud. Persian Jewry used simple brass cups, adding one each day. Although not much is known of the Jews of Cochin, India, their *ḥanukkiot* seem to be a blending of Sephardic and Indian influences. In any form, the *m'norah* remains a symbol of faith triumphing over religious persecution.

Tradition still dictates that the eight candles must be on the same level, with no one candle higher than another, because each day of Ḥanukkah is equally important. *Ḥanukkiot*, customs, songs and prayers vary greatly among Jews from continent to continent, but the message of Ḥanukkah has withstood the test of time: our strength is in our diversity.

THE HOME CELEBRATION CHECKLIST

To celebrate Ḥanukkah at home, you will need:

- *Ḥanukkiah*—one or more to be lit by everyone present

- Candles—44 are necessary for each *ḥanukkiah* that will be lit during the eight days of the festival

- Toys, Games, Books*

- Holiday Decorations*

- Special Foods*

Refer to appropriate sections in this manual.

LIGHTING THE ḤANUKKAH CANDLES

Who lights the candles?

Anyone may kindle the *ḥanukkiah* on behalf of those present. However, it is a growing practice to allow everyone to light a candle or to provide each person with his own *ḥanukkiah.*

When are they lit?

The Ḥanukkah lights should be kindled as soon as possible after sunset. On Friday, light the

Hanukkah candles first and then light the Shabbat candles. On Saturday night, light the Havdalah candle first, then kindle the *hanukkiah*.

Where do you place the ḥanukkiah?

A traditional oil or candle-lit *ḥanukkiah* is used for ceremonial purposes and may be placed in the window if it is not a fire hazard. An additional electric one may be placed at a window visible from the street.

How do you light the candles?

Insert the candles from right to left (facing you). Light the *Shamash* first and use it to kindle the new candle added that evening. Then proceed from left to right, always lighting the new candle first. The same order applies if oil is used (olive oil is preferable since the original miracle involved olive oil).

What blessings are recited and when?

On the first night, all three of the blessings are said. On all other nights, only the first two blessings are recited.

BLESSINGS FOR LIGHTING THE ḤANUKKAH CANDLES

1. Blessed are You,
   O Lord, our God,
   King of the Universe,
   who has sanctified us
   with Your commandments and
   commanded us to kindle
   the Ḥanukkah lights.

   Barukh Atah Adonai
   Elohaynu Melekh ha'olam
   asher kiddshanu
   b'mitzvotav v'tzivanu
   l'hadlik ner shel Ḥanukkah.

   בָּרוּךְ אַתָּה יְיָ
   אֱלֹהֵינוּ מֶלֶךְ הָעוֹלָם
   אֲשֶׁר קִדְּשָׁנוּ בְּמִצְוֹתָיו וְצִוָּנוּ
   לְהַדְלִיק נֵר שֶׁל חֲנֻכָּה.

2. Blessed are You,
   O Lord, our God,
   King of the Universe,
   who performed miracles for our
   ancestors in days gone by
   in this season of the year.

   Barukh Atah Adonai
   Elohaynu Melekh ha'olam
   she'asah nissim la'avotaynu
   ba'yamim ha'hem
   baz'man hazeh.

   בָּרוּךְ אַתָּה יְיָ
   אֱלֹהֵינוּ מֶלֶךְ הָעוֹלָם
   שֶׁעָשָׂה נִסִּים לַאֲבוֹתֵינוּ
   בַּיָּמִים הָהֵם בַּזְּמַן הַזֶּה.

3. Blessed are You,
   O Lord, our God,
   King of the Universe,
   who has kept us in life and
   enabled us to reach this day.

   Barukh Atah Adonai
   Elohaynu Melekh ha'olam
   shehehe'yanu v'ki'manu
   v'higiyanu laz'man hazeh.

   בָּרוּךְ אַתָּה יְיָ
   אֱלֹהֵינוּ מֶלֶךְ הָעוֹלָם
   שֶׁהֶחֱיָנוּ וְקִיְּמָנוּ
   וְהִגִּיעָנוּ לַזְּמַן הַזֶּה.

SUGGESTED OUTLINE FOR AN ADDITIONAL HOME SERVICE

Assemble around the *ḥanukkiah* with the proper number of candles in place. Recite the traditional blessings, adding the following prayers on the appropriate nights.

For the Shamash
(recite each evening)

As one candle may kindle many others and yet lose none of its own light, so Judaism has kindled the light of truth for many religions in many lands and still shines brightly through the ages.

For the First Night
The first light tells us of Him whose first command was "let there be light." The darkness of idol worship and immorality was scattered when Israel brought radiant knowledge of one God.

For the Second Night
The second light is the light of Torah. Israel's Book of Law has brought learning and truth to all of the Western World. "The Commandment is a lamp and the Law is a light."

For the Third Night
The third light is the light of Justice. No nation can endure that which is unjust to the weak. "Justice, always justice, shalt thou pursue!"

For the Fourth Night
The fourth light is the light of Mercy. Cruelty hardens the heart and destroys friendship. "Do justice and love mercy."

For the Fifth Night
The fifth light is the light of Holiness. Purity of thought; nobility of action make all of life sacred. "Holy, Holy, Holy is the Lord of Hosts; the whole earth is filled with His glory."

For the Sixth Night
The sixth light is the light of Love. When the love which our parents give us makes all of our life beautiful, we learn to understand the Biblical work. "Thou shalt love the Lord thy God with all thy heart and soul and might."

For the Seventh Night
The seventh light is the calm light of Patience. Nothing can be achieved in haste. The spreading tree and the soul of man grow slowly to perfection. Thus sang King David, "Trust in the Lord, wait patiently for Him."

For the Eighth Night
The eighth light is the light of courage. Let truth and justice be your armor, and fear not. Judah Maccabee, the hero of Ḥanukkah, lived by the words Moses spoke to Joshua, "Be strong and of good courage."

GIFT-GIVING

A favorite holiday tradition is the giving of gifts to children, who eagerly look forward to receiving toys, games and *"gelt".* The presentation of money to celebrate Ḥanukkah is rooted in the age old story of the Maccabees. Some 25 years after the rededication of the Temple, the Jews (led by the eldest son of Mattathias) were permitted to mint their own coins, a gesture which symbolized the legal recognition of their independence. Through the years the giving of coins has become associated with the Ḥanukkah holiday. It is now customary to give real money or imitation gold coins made of foil-covered chocolate. The government of Israel produces a special coin each year to commemorate Ḥanukkah.

Floating M'norah by Emil Shenfeld, sterling silver-plate, signed and numbered, Israel, 1986.

Tz'dakah Box by Leonard Meiselman and Shirley Kagan, sterling silver-plate, Italy, 1988.

Dreidel by Yossi Nataf, sterling silver, Israel, 1987.

Courtesy of In The Spirit Studio, New York.

In an essay entitled *"Yes, Virginia, There Is A Ḥanukkah"*, Rabbi Perry Raphael Rank advises parents that Ḥanukkah gift-giving ought to remind children that Ḥanukkah is a holiday in which we take pride in our identity as Jews. Among the significant gifts that might be given to family and friends are *m'zuzzot, hallah* covers, candlesticks, *tallitot,* Jewish art and Jewish books. The holiday should be used to reinforce the most glorious of Jewish traditions: Talmud Torah—the study of Torah. Every Jewish child should have his own Bible and *Siddur.*

Doll House Ḥanukkah Lamp silver, Eastern Europe, early 19th century. Bequest of Judge Irving Lehman, 1945. Courtesy of Congregation Emanu-El Museum, New York. Photograph by Will Brown.

27

At least one gift-purchasing expedition should be a family outing to the Synagogue Judaica Shop to purchase a new *ḥanukkiah*. If you already have one, why not start a collection? The many contemporary designs are outstanding statements of Jewish artistic expression. A *ḥanukkiah* on view in the breakfront year-round is a powerful reminder of Jewish identity.

As a child leaves for school or to live on his own, the family can make a significant statement by presenting him with a *ḥanukkiah*. A Ḥanukkah *m'norah* and a pair of Shabbat candlesticks become a meaningful holiday or graduation gift for any young adult.

Yet another way to reinterpret gift-giving in a Jewish context is to give *tz'dakah*. Establish a Ḥanukkah savings account or a special *"pushke"*. On the last night of the holiday, count the money and decide which charities will be the beneficiaries.

The Jewish gifts we give will remind everyone that Ḥanukkah is neither a birthday party nor a Jewish Christmas! The purpose of Ḥanukkah gift-giving is to reinforce Jewish values and traditions.

Games and Activities

*P*ositive, exciting images of our Jewish heritage can be projected through games, crafts and decorations highlighting the Ḥanukkah holiday.

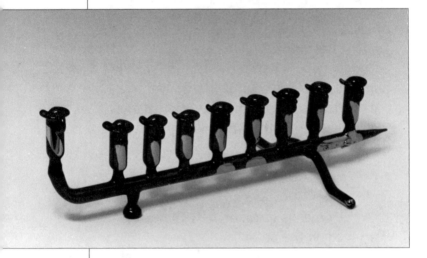

Games

DREIDEL:

Glass M'norah— by J. Stien, blown glass with 23K gold. Judaica Exchange, Monsey, New York.

The most popular game associated with Ḥanukkah is *dreidel* or *s'vivon*, probably derived from an old German gambling game. It is played with a four-sided top, on each side of which is one of four letters: נ *(nun)*, ג *(gimmel)*, ה *(hay)* and

שׁ (shin). Although these represent various gambling terms, they have been reinterpreted to mean " נֵס גָּדוֹל הָיָה שָׁם " — "a great miracle happened there." In Gematria, these letters have the numerical equivalent of 358, which is the same as " מָשִׁיחַ " — "Messiah," as well as the phrase " יְיָ מֶלֶךְ יְיָ מָלָךְ יְיָ יִמְלֹךְ " — "God is King, God was King, God will be King."

HOW TO PLAY DREIDEL

At least two players are needed to begin. Everyone in the game starts with 10 or 15 pennies, nuts, raisins, etc. Each player puts one of these in the middle (called the pot). The dreidel is spun by one player at a time. When the dreidel stops spinning, the letter that ends up on top indicates whether the player will give to or take from the pot.

Nun means *nisht* or "nothing". The player does nothing.

Gimmel means *gantz* or "all". The player takes everything in the pot.

Hay means *halb* or "half". The player takes half of what is in the pot.

Shin means *shtel* or "put in". The player adds an object to the pot.

When only one object or none is left in the pot, every player adds one. When an odd number of objects are in the pot, the player rolling *hay* (half) takes half the total plus one. When one person has won everything, the game is over.

DREIDEL VARIATIONS:

MUSICAL DREIDEL—Seat the children in a circle. While someone sings a Ḥanukkah song or plays a record or tape, the children pass the dreidel from one to another. When the music stops, the one left holding the dreidel is eliminated. Continue until only one person remains as the winner.

CALL DREIDEL—The object of this game is for the players to call out the letter on which the dreidel will fall. Each player gets a chance to spin the dreidel. The calling is done before the dreidel is spun. Keep a scorecard; on each round, each one who guesses correctly gets a point. The game ends when one of the players reaches 15 points.

FOR PRE-SCHOOLERS:

ḤANUKKAH FINGER PLAY— Make a face on each finger of a glove to represent the five Maccabee brothers. Make Antiochus and Mattathias from two socks or mittens. Using these as puppets, tell the story of Ḥanukkah to the little ones, having each son bow to the father, the father gesture to the son, and so forth.

Wooden Dreidels carved wood, Poland, 18th century. The Rose and Benjamin Mintz Collection, The Jewish Museum, New York.

WORD PLAY:

ḤANUKKAH SCRAMBLE—Prepare sheets of paper with lists of Ḥanukkah characters, foods, games and symbols. Scramble the letters and give children a time limit (suggested—10 minutes) to unscramble them. Award a prize to the one with the largest number of correct answers.

1. RANHOM (M'NORAH)
2. TAIATASHMT (MATTATHIAS)
3. LANDSEC (CANDLES)
4. NAHMONEAS (HASMONEAN)
5. BECAMACES (MACCABEES)
6. HAKANHUK (HANUKKAH)
7. LERIDED (DREIDEL)
8. KESLAT (LATKES)
9. SUCHOINAT (ANTIOCHUS)
10. SYNAIRS (SYRIANS)

ḤANUKKAH WORD GAME—Give each player a pencil and a sheet of paper on which the word ḤANUKKAH has been written. Children write down all of the words they can form from the letters of Ḥanukkah. No letter may be used in any word more times than it appears in Ḥanukkah. Set a time limit; the one who records the most words wins.

ḤANUKKAH GUESSING—In a box in the center of a table place several cards, on each of which is written the name of one of the Ḥanukkah characters or objects. Each player takes a card and, without mentioning the name aloud, writes two sentences about the name found on it. The sentences are then read aloud. All try to guess who or what is being described.

MORE ACTIVE ACTIVITIES:

ḤANUKKAH PEANUT HUNT—

On 8 peanuts, write the letter H

On 8 more, the letter A

On 4, the letter N

On 4, the letter U

On 8, the letter K

The lettered peanuts total 32. To make the game more difficult, include some peanuts with no letters. Hide the peanuts in a limited area. Set a time limit and give the signal to begin the hunt. At the end of the allotted time, 5 points are given to the player having the most peanuts and 7 for each group of peanuts that spells "Ḥanukkah". The one with the highest score wins the prize.

ḤANUKKAH BOWLING—Put several large blocks in a straight line. The block in the center represents King Antiochus. The other blocks are his soldiers. Children stand ten paces away, roll a ball and try to hit the king and his soldiers.

ADDITIONAL ACTIVITIES:

1. Listen to a Ḥanukkah story.

2. Make holiday cards and/or tape songs to be sent to children in other countries and to distant relatives and friends.

3. "A GIFT OF TIME"—Instead of giving a different gift each night, family members and friends present each other with pages showing pictures of things that they promise to do during the coming year. Parents can promise activities such as baking cookies together, going on a picnic or attending a ball game. Children can promise to help with the dishes, rake the lawn or baby sit for younger siblings. On the last night, the pages are bound together in a booklet with "coupons" that can be redeemed at a later date.

Crafts

ḤANUKKIAH: The *M'norah* used for the ceremonial candle lighting should be as large and as beautiful as possible. What shape should it be? As long as the flames are kept at an even height and do not merge to form one fire, one has a choice of shapes: straight line, semicircle, curve, etc. The *Shamash* must be distinguishable from the other candles and may be placed higher.

Ḥanukkiot can be made of properly treated clay, wooden spools, or soapstone. More ambitious craftsmen may choose to create ḥanukkiot from wood, tile, metal, glass or other media.

PLACEMATS: To make your own Ḥanukkah placemats, laminate any holiday design printed on paper between two pieces of 5-mil plastic sheets. Plastic laminating material can be purchased at hobby shops.

STAINED GLASS WINDOW: Create a "stained glass" window from colored cellophane paper outlined with black construction paper. The illustration can be a Ḥanukkah greeting or a picture with a holiday motif.

Traveling Oil M'norah by Arie Salomon and Shirley Kagan, brass, 1990. In he Spirit Studio, New York.

Decorations

Ornamental *ḥanukkiot* can be made of a variety
of materials, such as wood or wire covered
with ribbon, foil or flowers. Cutouts of construction or craft paper can be used for wall
decorations, party invitations or place cards.
A pattern can be made of cardboard and the
outline traced on paper for cutting. Involve
family and friends in the decorating process.
Mobiles, daisy chains, cutouts, napkins and
streamers are examples of decorations that are
easy to create. Decorations will be more effective
if a central motif is used throughout.

Suggestions include:

SYMBOLS:
    Ḥanukkiot and candles
    Hammers (used in battle by Eleazar)
    Elephants (which the Syrians rode)
    Stars of David
    Lions of Judah
    Dreidels
    Bows (used in battle)

COLORS:
    Blue and white (as in the Israeli flag)
    Yellow or gold (for Lion of Judah, Star of David
      or *ḥanukkiot)*
    Silver (for elephants, bows, stars or dreidels)

To order games, toys and activity books,
refer to **Media and Resource Guide.**

Music

Ma - oz tzur y' - shu - a - ti l' - kha na - eh l' sha - be - ah
Rock of Ag - es, let our song praise Thy sav - ing pow - er;

ti - kon bet t' - fi - la - ti v' - sham to - dah n' za - be - ah l' -
thou a - midst the rag - ing foes wast our shelt' - ring tow - er.

-et ta - khin mat - be - ah mi - tzar ham - na - be - ah
Fu - rious they as - sailed us, but Thine arm a - vail - ed us,

az eg - mor b' - shir miz - mor ha - nuk - kat ha - miz - be - ah.
And Thy word broke their sword when our own strength failed us.

MA-OZ TZUR

Ma-oz tzur y'shu-ati
'kha na-eh l'sha-be-ah
'i-kon bet t'fi-lati
'sham to-dah n'za-be-ah

'et ta-khin mat-be-ah
Mi-tzar ha-m'na-be-ah
Az eg-mor b'shir mizmor
Ha-nu-kkat ha-miz-be-ah.

ROCK OF AGES

Rock of ages, let our song
Praise Thy saving power
Thou amidst the raging foes
Wast our sheltering tower
Furious they assailed us
But Thine arm availed us
And Thy word
Broke their sword
When our own strength failed us.

WHO CAN RETELL?

Who can retell the things that befell us
Who can count them?
In every age a hero or sage
Came to our aid!
Ah, at this time of year in days of yore
Maccabees the Temple did restore
And today our people as we dreamed
Through their faith and courage are redeemed!

ḤANUKKAH O ḤANUKKAH

Ḥa-nu-kkah, O Ḥa-nu-kkah!
Come light the m'no-rah.
Let's have a party,
We'll all dance the hora
Gather 'round the table
We'll give you a treat,
S'vi-vo-nim to play with
L'vi-vot to eat.

And while we are playing
The candles are burning low.
*One for each night,
They shed a sweet light
To remind us of days long ago. (Repeat from *)

MY DREIDEL

I have a little dreidel,
I made it out of clay
And when it's dry and ready
Then dreidel I shall play.

Chorus:
O dreidel, dreidel, dreidel!
I made it out of clay.
O dreidel, dreidel, dreidel
Now dreidel I shall play.

It has a lovely body,
With leg so short and thin
And when it is all tired,
It drops and then I win.

S'VI-VON

S'vi-von, sov, sov, sov!
Ḥa-nu-kkah hu ḥag tov!
Ḥa-nu-kkah hu ḥag tov!
S'vi-von, sov, sov!

Ḥag sim-ḥah hu la-am
Nes ga-dol ha-yah sham
Nes ga-dol ha-yah sham
Ḥag sim-ḥah hu la-am.

Holiday Fare—
Favorite Recipes

ᴸATKES

Latkes made from grated raw potatoes are traditionally served on Ḥanukkah by Ashkenazi Jews. Zucchini, cheese and corn latkes are appealing alternatives. Israeli *sufganiyot*, *pashtida* and *birmuelos*, popular among Sephardic Jews, are interesting additions to Ḥanukkah meals.

HELPFUL HINTS

• For light and fluffy latkes: grate the onion first, then the potatoes.

• Add a pinch of baking soda to the mixture to keep it white.

• Fry in hot oil.

• Turn only once.

• Do not crowd latkes in the pan.

• Drain on paper towels.

• Latkes are best served hot from the frying pan. To rewarm, place on baking rack over a cookie sheet in a hot oven.

• To freeze fried latkes: After draining on paper towels, place on cookie trays. Flash freeze (place uncovered in freezer). Put batches of frozen latkes in sealed plastic freezer bags and return to the freezer. Do not defrost. Reheat in a pre-heated hot (400°) oven.

KUGELS

As an alternative to frying, any of the latke recipes may be baked in well-greased baking pans or muffin tins at 350º until done.

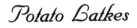

Potato Latkes

4 large potatoes	1 tsp. salt
1 tsp. grated onion	Dash of pepper
1 egg	1 tsp. baking powder
2 Tbsp. flour (heaping)	Oil for frying

Grate unpeeled potatoes on a fine grater (in a food processor, cut potatoes into chunks; use shredder blade). Drain through a sieve. Add onion, beaten egg, and remaining ingredients and mix. Heat ¼" oil in frying pan to 375°. Drop batter by rounded tablespoons into hot pan. Flatten with spatula. Fry until crisp and brown on each side. Drain on paper towels. Serve hot with sour cream, jam, applesauce, or cinnamon and sugar. Serves 4–6.

Apple Latkes (D)

2 large tart apples (cored, not peeled, chopped into ½" chunks)
¼ cup brown sugar
¼ tsp. cinnamon
1½ cups flour (sifted)
1 Tbsp. sugar
1 tsp. baking powder
Kosher salt to taste
1 egg (beaten)
1 cup milk
1 Tbsp. butter (melted)
Oil for frying

Combine apples with brown sugar and cinnamon; set aside. In a separate bowl, mix together flour, sugar, baking powder and salt. Combine egg, milk and butter and stir into flour mixture to form a thin batter. Fold in apple mixture. In a large frying pan, heat ¼" oil to 375°. Pour in ¼ cup batter for each latke. Flatten each with a spatula and fry until lightly brown. Turn carefully to brown on the other side. Drain on paper towel. Serve with sour cream or combination of 1 Tbsp. cinnamon and ½ cup sugar. Yields about 12 medium-sized pancakes.

Zucchini Latkes (D)

2 small zucchini
(unpeeled, grated
and drained)
Kosher salt to taste
3 Tbsp. matzah meal

3 Tbsp. pot cheese
Freshly ground pepper
1 egg (beaten)
Oil for frying

Combine zucchini and remaining ingredients. In a large frying pan heat ¼" oil to 375°. Drop by tablespoons into pan. Flatten with spatula. Brown on both sides. Drain on paper towels. Serve hot. Serves 4.

NOTE: Do not use a blender. It makes the mixture too watery.

Corn Latkes

1 can cream style
corn (drained)
2 eggs (beaten)
1 tsp. baking powder

2 Tbsp. flour (heaping)
1 tsp. sugar
½ tsp. salt
Oil for frying

Mix all ingredients together. In a large frying pan heat ¼" oil to 375°. Drop batter by spoonfuls and flatten with a spatula. Brown on both sides, drain on towels and serve hot. May be served with maple syrup. Serves 4.

Potato-Zucchini Pancakes

1 medium zucchini (about ½ pound grated and drained)
1 large Idaho potato (about 10 ounces, grated and drained)
3 Tbsp. very finely minced scallions
1 Tbsp. finely minced fresh dill
1 egg (lightly beaten)
3 Tbsp. flour
Salt to taste
Freshly ground black pepper to taste
Vegetable oil for frying

Mix potato and zucchini together. Add scallions, dill, egg, flour, salt and pepper. Mix well. Heat ¼" oil in frying pan. Drop by tablespoons and flatten. Fry until golden brown on each side. Drain pancakes on paper towels and serve hot. May be served with freshly grated Parmesan cheese, plain yogurt or sour cream. Yields about 16 three inch pancakes.

Pineapple Fritters (D)

1 cup flour
2 tsp. baking powder
¼ tsp. salt
2 Tbsp. sugar
2 Tbsp. melted butter
1 egg (beaten)
⅓ to ½ cup milk

1 dozen slices of
canned pineapple or
2 cups of canned
pineapple chunks
(drained)
Oil for frying

To prepare the batter, stir together the flour, baking powder, salt and sugar. Combine the egg, milk, and melted butter and stir into the dry ingredients. Blend until smooth but do not over-beat. Batter should be heavy enough to coat the fruit; if it is not, adjust with more milk or flour to proper consistency. Dip pineapple rings into batter or stir two cups of pineapple cubes into batter. Deep fry in hot oil until well browned. Drain on paper towels. Serve hot. May be sprinkled with confectioners sugar. Yields 12 fritters.

Sweet Potato Latkes

6 medium sweet potatoes	¼ tsp. cinnamon
6 oz. Tofutti Egg Watchers™	¼ tsp. white pepper
	1½ tsp. salt
4 green onions (diced)	2 Tbsp. all-purpose flour
	1 tsp. garlic (minced)
2 Tbsp. honey	½ cup bread crumbs
	Vegetable oil for frying

Peel potatoes and shred in food processor on smallest grating blade. In a large bowl, combine Egg Watchers, green onion, honey, garlic, cinnamon, white pepper, salt, flour and bread crumbs; mix with potatoes. Work the mixture in your hands until it is thickened. Form into 2—3 ounce patties and press thin. In skillet, heat ¼" oil until hot; fry patties until golden brown on both sides. Remove from pan and drain on paper towels. Serve hot. Yields about 20 latkes.

Tofu Latkes

1 pound tofu
8 oz. Tofutti Egg
  Watchers™
½ cup flour (for
  crunchier latkes,
  use ½ cup matzah
  meal instead)

1 Tbsp. lemon juice
Salt and pepper to
  taste
Pinch of garlic, minced
Vegetable oil for frying

Combine tofu and Egg Watchers in blender. While blending add flour, lemon juice and seasonings; process until mixture is smooth. Heat ¼" oil to 375° in a large heavy skillet. For each latke, drop 2 Tbsp. of the mixture into pan; fry until golden brown on both sides. Drain on paper towels and serve hot. Yields 12 medium sized latkes.

Variation: By hand, add ½ cup frozen, thawed chopped spinach or broccoli to the mixture after blending.

Israeli Pashtida (Fried Potato Kugel)

5 medium potatoes
(grated and drained)
2 onions (grated
and drained)
2 eggs (beaten)

2 Tbsp. matzah meal
Dash of black pepper
Margarine or oil for
frying

Mix potatoes and onions and add remaining ingredients. Pour all batter into a well-greased 10" frying pan and fry on a low flame for 20–25 minutes. Loosen sides and turn over carefully onto a large plate. Invert so that the raw side is on top. Place back in the frying pan with the raw side down. Fry on low flame for an additional 20–25 minutes. Yields 4–6 portions.

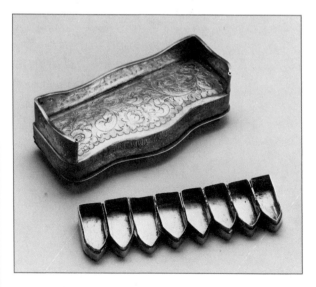

Caribbean Hanukkah Lamp embossed and chased silver, early 18th century. Gift of Dr. and Mrs. Frederick Greenwald, The National Museum of American Jewish History, Philadelphia. Photograph by Will Brown.

49

Turkish Birmuelos

2 packages dry yeast
3 cups warm water
2 Tbsp. sugar
½ tsp. salt
2 Tbsp. vegetable oil

6½ cups flour
6 cups vegetable oil
for frying
Confectioners sugar
or honey

Combine yeast, water and sugar. Let stand for 10 minutes until mixture foams. Add salt, 2 Tbsp. oil and flour. Mix well to make a smooth, sticky dough. Cover the bowl with a clean cloth and allow the dough to rise in a warm place for 1 hour or until it doubles in size. Punch down the dough. Allow to rise for an additional 30 minutes. While dough is rising for the second time, heat oil in deep sauce pan to 375°. Break off 2 inch balls of dough and drop them into hot oil, a few at a time. Turn when golden on one side. When golden on the other side, remove and drain on paper towels. Sprinkle with confectioners sugar or honey and serve hot.

Sufganiyot (Israeli Filled Doughnuts) (D)

2½ cups flour
2 cups hot milk
2 packages yeast
¼ cup lukewarm milk
6 egg yolks
⅔ cup sugar
1 tsp. vanilla

Rind of 1 lemon or
  orange (grated)
½ cup butter
Jam for filling
Oil for frying
Confectioners sugar

Sift one cup of flour into the hot milk and beat until smooth, then allow to cool. Dissolve the yeast in the lukewarm milk, add to the flour mixture, and set aside for about half an hour.

Mix the egg yolks and sugar with the vanilla and rind and add to the dough. Then add the remaining flour and the butter and knead until smooth and shiny. Place in a greased bowl and invert the dough so top is shiny. Cover with a towel. Allow to rise in a draft free area until double in bulk (about 45 minutes).

Roll out on a floured board to a thickness of ½ inch and cut into rounds. Put a teaspoon of jam in the center of one round and cover with another round. Press the edges together and allow to rise again in a warm place. Fry in ¼" hot oil, drain on paper towels and dust with confectioners sugar.

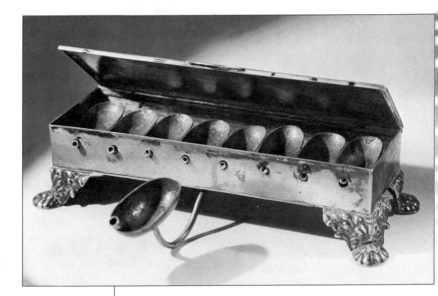

BAKING FOR HANUKKAH

Bake your favorite cake recipe in a square or oblong pan. Cut the cake into the shape of a star of David, frost with white icing and outline the star in blue icing.

Decorative Icing

½ cup pareve margarine

1 cup confectioners sugar

1 tsp. flavoring (lemon, vanilla, etc.)

Cream margarine and add sugar gradually; add flavoring and mix. Optional: tint frosting with vegetable coloring.

52

Ḥanukkah Cookies

½ cup butter or margarine
1 cup sugar
1 tsp. vanilla

1 ½ cups flour
1 ½ tsp. baking powder
¼ tsp. salt
1 egg

Combine butter and sugar in a bowl, mixing until smooth. Add egg and vanilla and mix well. Sift flour, baking powder and salt into another bowl. Add half the flour mixture to the butter mixture and stir. Add the rest of the flour mixture. If dough is too sticky, add more flour. Form dough into a ball and wrap in waxed paper. Refrigerate for at least one hour.

Preheat oven to 350°. Roll out dough on floured board or table. Cut with Ḥanukkah cookie cutters. If you don't have any, cut out cardboard dreidel and star shapes and use them as a guide to cut the dough. Place on ungreased cookie sheet and bake for 8–10 minutes. Yields 3–4 dozen cookies.

Study Guide

A major feat of the Maccabees was the triumph of a Jewish way of life over Hellenism. This struggle is still being fought today, particularly in any home where a child would rather

play sports than attend Religious School, or an adult thinks that the study of Judaism is only for children. We enhance Jewish life when we take on Jewish study as a family activity of life-long importance. Ḥanukkah is a good time to begin to study together at home. Every Rabbi can suggest texts, stories and ethical tales that are appropriate for various age levels. Reading and discussing the Bible aloud is a good way to start.

M'norah by Robert Lipnick, ceramic, United States, 1980's. In The Spirit Studio, New York.

Ḥanukkah Quiz

QUESTIONS

1. In which Hebrew month does Ḥanukkah occur?

2. What does the word "Ḥanukkah" mean?

3. Most Jewish holidays have more than one name. What is another name for Ḥanukkah?

4. For how many days is Ḥanukkah observed?

5. What historical event does Ḥanukkah commemorate?

6. Approximately how long ago did the Maccabean struggle take place?
   (a) 3100 years ago
   (b) 2100 years ago
   (c) 1100 years ago

7. Who decreed the observance of Ḥanukkah?

8. By what name is the candle called which is used to light the others?

9. What unusual event is commemorated by kindling the Ḥanukkah lights?

10. According to Jewish religious law, there is a basic difference between Shabbat candles and Ḥanukkah lights which has nothing to do with size and color. What is that difference?

11. Unscramble these Hebrew words: *Gadol Sham Ha'yah Nes.* What do they mean?

12. By what special name was Antiochus IV, King of the Syrian Greeks, called?
    (a) Euphrates
    (b) Elephantine
    (c) Epimanes
    (d) Epiphanes

13. Who were the first Jewish leaders to raise the flag of rebellion against Antiochus?

14. One of the following names does not belong. Which one is it and why? Simon, Judah, Eleazar, Jonathan, Josephus.

15. In what town was the banner of revolt first unfurled?

16. What was Mattathias' inspiring call to the scattered forces of Israel?

17. What is the origin of the words of Mattathias' call?

18. What do the words *"Mi khamokha ba'aylim Adonai"* ("Who is like You, Oh Lord, among the mighty?") have to do with Ḥanukkah?

19. What do Hannah and Eleazar have in common?

20. What other famous Jewish woman is connected with Ḥanukkah?

21. True or false? The *Books of the Maccabees* and the *Book of Judith* are found in our Bible?

22. What is the name of the special prayer recited on Ḥanukkah?

23. What had the Syrian Greeks done to the Holy Temple in Jerusalem?

24. What is Ḥanukkah *"gelt"?*

25. What special foods are served during Ḥanukkah?

ANSWERS

1. Kislev

2. Dedication. Since the Holy Temple in Jerusalem had been dedicated many years before the time of the Maccabees, they are said to have "rededicated" it. Hence, Ḥanukkah is often referred to as the Holiday of Rededication. "Ḥanukkah" is also used in the Hebrew phrase equivalent to the English "housewarming". . ."Ḥanukkat HaBa'yit", literally, "Dedication of the Home."

3. *"Ḥag Ha'Urim"*—The Festival of Lights.

4. Eight Days. The eight-day period reminds us that the return to the Temple was intended to observe the holiday of Sukkot, which lasts for eight days.

5. The successful struggle for liberty carried on by the Jews under the Maccabees against their Syrian-Greek oppressors.

6. (b) 2100 years ago — 167-165 B.C.E.

7. Judah Maccabee and the Elders of Israel

8. *Shamash*

9. The miracle of the oil which was expected to keep the Eternal Light lit for only one day, yet miraculously lasted for eight days, long enough for fresh oil to be supplied.

10. Shabbat candles are for enjoyment, for light, for our benefit. Ḥanukkah candles are only for commemorating the miracle.

11. *"Nes Gadol Ha'yah Sham"* — "A great miracle happened there." The first letter of each of these words corresponds to the Hebrew letters on dreidels made outside Israel. The Israeli dreidel has *"Nes Gadol Ha'yah Poh"* — "A great miracle happened HERE."

12. (d) Epiphanes, the "illustrious". Jewish punsters called him Epimanes, the "madman".

13. Mattathias and his five sons.

14. Josephus does not belong. He was a Jewish pro-Graeco-Roman historian; the others were four of the sons of Mattathias, the fifth being Yohanan.

15. Modi'in, a village northwest of Jerusalem in the foothills of Judea.

16. *"Mi L'Adonai Aylai"* — "Whoever is on the side of God, follow me!"

17. Moses used them to rally those faithful to the Lord against the golden calf *(Exodus 32:26)*.

18. Moses first uttered them after the miracle of the Sea of Reeds. They were used as the inscription on Judah Maccabee's banner. The initial letters in this Hebrew verse make up the word MKBI — Maccabee. Some, however, derive the name "Maccabee" from the Hebrew word *"Makkeb"* which means "Hammer", *"Mazbi"* which means "General" or *"Makkabiah"* which means "Named by the Lord".

19. They were both martyrs for their religion, whose stories are told in the *Books of the Maccabees.* Hannah was the heroic woman who was willing to see her seven sons killed rather than worship idols. Eleazar was an old man who would not heed the tyrant King's demands and was put to death.

20. Judith, whose story is told in the *Apocrypha.* She was a descendant of the Maccabees who overcame Holofernes, the powerful enemy leader, thus saving her people.

21. False. They are found in the literary collection known as the *Apocrypha*, books not accepted for inclusion in the Bible.

22. *"Al HaNissim"* — "For the Miracles". (*"Hallel"* is also recited.)

23. It was converted into a sanctuary of Jupiter the Olympian, and a statue of the god was erected. The Temple was filled with riot and revelry; heathen sacrifices were offered and swine's blood was poured on the altar.

24. Coins (money) given to the children as gifts on Ḥanukkah to remind us of the coins struck by the Maccabees after their victory, signifying their freedom from the tyrant.

25. *Latkes (l'vivot)*; in English, pancakes. In Israel, jelly doughnuts *(sufganiyot)* are also eaten, because the great amount of oil needed to make them is reminiscent of the miracle of the oil.

Contemporary Hanukkah coins feature designs inspired by ancient Judean coins. Minted by Government of Israel, Jerusalem.

QUESTIONS TO TRIGGER DISCUSSION

1. Is Ḥanukkah a major or a minor festival on the Jewish calendar? How can one tell, in terms of the nature of the observance of a festival, whether this is a major festival?

2. Is there a parallel between the desire to adopt Hellenistic customs and characteristics during the time of the Ḥanukkah story and the lure of secularism today?

3. Should one send Ḥanukkah gifts to non-Jewish friends and relatives? Should one send Christmas gifts to non-Jewish friends and relatives?

4. Should the history and customs of Ḥanukkah be taught in public schools? Should Jewish communities erect *hanukkiot* in public areas?

5. Is Ḥanukkah "the Jewish Christmas?" Is this a "harmless" designation?

6. How can a parent of young children counter the prevalence of Christmas? To what extent should Jewish children be permitted to participate in school and community Christmas celebrations?

Media and Resource Guide

Books

GENERAL

CHILDREN'S

PRE-SCHOOL

Media

VIDEO AND FILM

RECORDS AND CASSETTES

Women's League Scripts

Women's League Artforms

63

Books: General

Encyclopedia Judaica, "Hanukkah", "Hanukkah Lamps" Vol.7

Hanukkah Anthology by Philip Goodman; Jewish Publication Society, Philadelphia

Hanukkah: Eight Nights, Eight Lights by Malka Drucker; Holiday House

Hanukkah Resource Manual; Board of Jewish Education of Greater New York

Holiday Tales of Sholom Aleichem, Stories of Chanukah, Passover and Other Jewish Holidays; Scribners, NY

Hanukkah Lamp by Mae Shafter Rockland, wood covered in fabric with molded plastic figures, Princeton, New Jersey, 1974. The Jewish Museum, New York.

My Glorious Brothers by Howard Fast;
Jordan Publishing, NY

**Seasons of Our Joy, A Handbook of the
Jewish Festivals** by Arthur I. Waskow;
Summit Books, NY

**The Complete Family Guide to Jewish
Holidays** by Dalia Hardof Renberg;
Adama Books, NY

The First Jewish Catalog by Richard Siegel,
Michael Strassfeld, Sharon Strassfeld; Jewish
Publication Society, Philadelphia

The Hanukkah Book by Mae Shafter Rockland;
Schocken Books, NY

The Jewish Holidays, A Guide and Commentary
by Michael Strassfeld, Harper and Row, NY

**The Jewish Party Book, A Contemporary
Guide to Customs and Crafts** by May Shafter
Rockland; Schocken Books, NY

The Power of Light, Eight Stories for Hanukkah
by Isaac Bashevis Singer; Farrar Strauss
(hardcover), Avon (paperback)

The Songs of Hanukkah compiled by Ḥazzan
Sidney G. Rabinowitz; Women's League for
Conservative Judaism, NY

Books: Children

A Hanukkah Letter from Moscow
Activity Book by Jeffrey S. Winter, PhD;
Contemporary Designs, Gilbert, Iowa

All About Hanukkah by Judye Groner and
Madeline Wikler, illustrated by Rosalyn
Schanzer; Kar-Ben Publishing, Rockville, MD

All About Hanukkah in Story and Song
Story narrated by Penninah Schram, favorite
songs by Margie Rosenthal and Ilene Safyan;
Kar-Ben Copies, Rockville, MD

Festival of Lights—The Story of Hanukkah
Retold by Maida Silverman, illustrated by
Carolyn S. Ewing; Simon and Schuster, NY

Hanukkiyah for Dina by Floreva G. Cohen;
Board of Jewish Education of Greater New York

Holiday Adventures of Achbar by Barbara
Sofer, illustrated by Nina Gaelen; Kar-Ben
Copies, Rockville, MD

I Can Celebrate by Ann Eisenberg; Kar-Ben
Copies, Rockville, MD

It's Hanukkah by Ellie Gellman, illustrated by
Katherine Kahn; Kar-Ben Copies, Rockville, MD

Jewish Days and Holidays Illustrated by Alona
Frankel; Adama Books, NY

Jewish Holiday Fun by Judith Hoffman Corwin; Julian Messner Publishers

Jewish Holiday Fun: A Workbook by David A. Adler; Kar-Ben Publishing, Rockville, MD

K'tonton in the Circus: A Hanukkah Adventure by Sadie Rose Weilerstein, illustrated by Marilyn Hirsch; Jewish Publication Society, Philadelphia

Malke's Secret Recipe: A Chanukah Story by David Adler, illustrated by Joan Halpern; Kar-Ben Copies, Rockville, MD

Miracle Meals: Eight Nights of Food 'N Fun for Chanukah by Madeline Wikler and Judyth Groner, illustrated by Chari Radin; Kar-Ben Copies, Rockville, MD

My Very Own Animated Jewish Holiday Activity Book Shapolsky Publishers, NY

Potato Pancakes All Around Written and illustrated by Marilyn Hirsch; Jewish Publication Society, Philadelphia

Rainbow Candles by Myra Shostak, illustrated by Katherine Kahn; Kar-Ben Copies, Rockville, MD

Hanukkah Lamp cast brass, Morocco, 8th-20th century. Gift of Dr. Harry ?. Friedman, The Jewish Museum, New York.

Sifron Hanukkah Activity Workbook; Board of Jewish Education of Greater New York

The Animated Menorah, Travels on a Space Dreidel by Rony Oren and Ephraim Sidon; Scopus Films; Board of Jewish Education of Greater New York

The Best of K'tonton by Sadie Rose Weilerstein, illustrated by Marilyn Hirsch, introduction by Francine Klagsbrun; Jewish Publication Society, Philadelphia

The Children's Holiday Kitchen by Joan Nathan; Schocken Books, NY

The Modi'in Motel by Deborah Miller and Karen Ostrove; Kar-Ben Publishing, Rockville, MD

The Odd Potato by Eileen Sherman, illustrated by Katherine Kahn; Kar-Ben Copies, Rockville, MD

Treasures of Hanukkah Edited by Jean L. Scrocco, illustrated by Greg Hildebrandt; The Unicorn Publishing House, Morris Plains, NJ

Books: Pre-school

A Picture Book of Hanukkah by David A. Adler; Holiday House

Hanukkah Cat by Chaya Burstein; Kar-Ben Publishing Co.

Hanukkah, Eight Nights, Eight Lights by Malka Drucker; Holiday House

It's Chanukah by Ellie Gellman, illustrated by Katherine Kahn; Kar-Ben Copies, Rockville, MD

Let's Play Dreidel by Roz Grossman and Gladys Gerwirtz, illustrated by Sally Springer; songs recorded by Frances Goldman; Kar-Ben Copies, Rockville, MD

Nathan's Hanukkah Bargain by Jacqueline Dembar Greene; Kar-Ben Publishing Co.

The Hanukkah Tooth by Jacqueline Dembar Greene; Pascal Publishing

The Story of Chanukah for Children by Beverly Rae Charette; Ideals (Random House)

What Do You Do On A Jewish Holiday? Hanukkah Pop-up Book by Sol Scharfstein; KTAV Publishing, NY

Books: To Order

Contemporary Designs
213 Main Street
Gilbert, Iowa 50105

Kar-Ben Publishing Co.
6800 Tildenwood Lane
Rockville, MD 20852
(301) 984-8733; (1-800) 4-KARBEN

KTAV Publishing Company
120 East Broadway
New York, NY 10002

Board of Jewish Education
  of Greater New York
426 West 58th Street
New York, NY 10019

The Dreidel Factory
#1 Hazel Road
Berkeley, CA 94705
(415) 549-0379

The Israel Educational Materials
  and Games Center
c/o Israel Trade Center
111 West 40th Street
New York, NY 10018

Shapolsky Great Judaica
136 West 22nd Street
New York, NY 10011
(212) 633-2022

The Jewish Publication Society
1930 Chestnut Street
Philadelphia, PA 19103
(1-800) 234-3151

Torah Toys
1570 East Edinger Avenue
Santa Ana, CA 92705

Additional resources may be found in
Women's League's **Directories of Judaica
Shop Suppliers in North America and
in Israel.** Contact the National Education
Department to order.

*Electric M'norah
fiberoptic/lucite
electric,
Ben Ari Arts, LTD.,
New York.*

Media: Video and Film

A Cup of Light

Script by David Mark. A dramatization celebrating the festival of Ḥanukkah. The program deals with the history of several lamps, some dating back to the fourth century. It features Tom Bosley as narrator and selections by Yaffa Yarkoni, noted Israeli vocalist. *(Eternal Light/ Alden—rental; 30 min., B&W)*

A Hanukkah Celebration (Candle Unto Candle)

A delightful introduction to the Festival of Lights. We learn about many of the symbols of Ḥanukkah, how Soviet Jews celebrate this holiday of freedom, and how oil was prepared for the Temple in Jerusalem. Mike Burstyn and his puppet friends sing holiday songs and play dreidel. *(Ergo—purchase; 25 min., color)*

A Light in Darkness

Script by Joseph Mindel. Contemporary retelling of the Ḥanukkah story and the miraculous defeat of the vast Syrian forces by the Maccabees and their followers. *(BJE; Eternal Light/Alden—rental; 30 min., B&W)*

A Time for Valor

The story of Ḥanukkah with its struggle for freedom of worship is discussed by two boys who become closer by understanding the universal values of the holiday in the Ḥanukkah/Christmas season. *(Alden— rental; 13 1/2 min., B&W, 16 mm)*

Benjamin and the Miracle of Hanukkah

This charming animated Ḥanukkah video for younger children tells of the arduous journey of a young boy sent by Judah Maccabee to obtain oil for the Temple in Jerusalem. It deals with traditional values of the festival—the quest for religious freedom and the triumph of faith. Narrated by Herschel Bernardi. *(Ergo — purchase; 24 min., color)*

By the Light of the Candles

This film brings to life the story of the Maccabean struggle. As a young boy gazes at *ḥanukkiyot* at the Bezalel National Art Museum in Jerusalem, we hear the voice of Judah Maccabee relating his story, which is visualized by means of original illustrations. *(Alden— rental; 18 min., color, 16mm and video).*

Cry A Warning

Script by Morton Wishengrad. This Ḥanukkah story takes place in the year 166 B.C.E., in the time of the Maccabees. It tells of a 12-year-old Jewish boy who, brought up and educated in the Greek tradition, joins the Hebrews in their fight for freedom. *(Eternal Light/Alden—rental; 30 min., B&W)*

Eenie's Kitchen

Chef Eenie Frost introduces us to traditional foods associated with particular holidays. For Ḥanukkah, Eenie prepares *latkes* and *sufganiyot. (Ergo-purchase; 29 min., color)*

Getting Ready for Hanukkah

Introduces the story and tradition of Ḥanukkah to young children. Filmstrip with script and resource guide. *(BJE—purchase; 25 min., color)*

Hanukkah

Shows how Ḥanukkah, the Festival of Lights, is celebrated in Israel; includes the historical background of the holiday. *(Alden — sale/rental; 14½ min., color, 16mm and video)*

Keepers of the Flame: A Hanukkah Celebration

Four young friends discover the history and meaning of Ḥanukkah and how it relates to life today. VHS #36-010, Filmstrip #34-200, Slides #34-210. *(BJE—purchase; 25 minutes, color)*

Lights (A Story of Hanukkah)

An animated fantasy-adventure which retells, in allegorical form, the story of Hanukkah and the miracle of the lights. Narrator Judd Hirsch and actors Leonard Nimoy and Paul Michael Glazer greatly add to the impact of the film. *(Ergo—sale; Alden—sale/rental; 30 min., color)*

Oil For But One Day

Script by Marc Siegel. A program of drama and songs celebrating Ḥanukkah, featuring Theodore Bikel. It dramatizes the faith and will of men in every land and in every century to sustain the light of freedom. *(Eternal Light/Alden—rental; 30 min., B&W)*

The Dreidel

An adorable animated story about a dreidel searching for a friend who will play with him on Ḥanukkah. Useful for teaching about the holiday and improving Hebrew listening comprehension in young children. *(BJE—purchase; 10 min., color)*

The Five Sons

Script by Howard Fast. A rehearsal of a traditional Ḥanukkah play is portrayed as a means of dramatizing the eternal values embodied in the holiday. A father's reaction to sending his son off to war—now or 2000 years ago—is conveyed by having the actors discuss the motivations of the characters of the play in rehearsal. *(Eternal Light/Alden—rental; 30 min., B&W)*

The Jewish Holidays Video Guide

An overview of Shabbat and major holidays for all ages. Includes background material. *(Master Digital—purchase; 75 min., color)*

The Legate

Script by Howard Fast. The drama, based on the book *My Glorious Brothers*, takes place in Jerusalem in the middle of the 2nd century B.C.E.. A legate is sent by Rome to conclude a treaty with the victorious Jewish leader, Simon Maccabeus, and to report on the ways of the Jews. *(Eternal Light/Alden—rental; 30 min., B&W)*

The Liberator

Script by Elihu Winer. This film blends narration with choral and solo music in explaining songs traditionally associated with the holiday as well as general music influenced by the theme of Ḥanukkah. *(Eternal Light/Alden—rental; 30 min., B&W)*

Media: Records and Cassettes

Ba Yamim HaHem BaZman HaZeh—Hanukkah Songs for Children by Shimon and Ilana; 16 songs in Hebrew and English (with transliteration). *Record #38-304, cassette #38-404. (BJE—purchase)*

Latkes and Hamantaschen by Fran Avni and Jacki Cytrynbaum; original songs, stories and narrative bring holidays to life for young children. *Record #38-310, cassette #38-410 (BJE- purchase)*

Alden Films *(sale/rental)*
Box 449
Clarksburg, NJ 08510
(201) 462-3522

Ergo Media *(sale only)*
P.O. Box 2037
Teaneck, NJ 07666
(201) 692-0404

Master Digital
8560 Sunset Boulevard
Los Angeles, CA 90069
(213) 659-4080

**Board of Jewish Education
 of Greater New York**
426 West 58th Street
New York, NY 10019
(212) 245-8200

**Eternal Light Film Library of the
 United Synagogue of America**
155 Fifth Avenue
New York, NY 10010
(212) 260-8450
(order from Alden Films; rental only)

Order by number from Women's League National Education Department.

To Light A Candle (103.2)

Depicts role of dedicated women; includes impressive candle-lighting ceremony (10 minutes)

No Strings Attached (103.11)

Two marionettes come alive, demand freedom, and then find that true freedom demands attachment to some strings, i.e., law and responsibility (20 minutes)

Miracles (103.13)

Eight "Miracles" explained in a song (20 minutes)

Victory Of The Spirit (103.14)

Modern version of the holiday story with characters from history (15 minutes)

Ḥanukkah Candle Lighting Ceremony (103.15)

The modern significance of each candle and the *Shamash* (less than 5 minutes)

Blame It On The Rabbi (103.16)

Light and amusing retelling of the Ḥanukkah story (10 minutes)

Women's League Artforms

Order by number from Women's League National Public Relations Department.

5731 #4 . . . "Celebrate With Us" Invitation

V49 . . . . Table Decorations

V258 . . . . . . Ḥanukkah Centerpieces

P261 . . . . . "Celebrate Ḥanukkah" Poster

V296 . . . . . . Candles as Table Decorations

#8 . . . . Poster/Border

#9 . . . . "Let's Celebrate" Invitation/Flyer

P180 . . . . . "Make It A Happy Holiday At Our. . ." Flyer

P184 . . . . . "It's A Family Affair" Invitation

Ḥanukkah Glossary

Ḥanukkah Lamp in the form of a Synagogue Facade cast, pierced and engraved brass, Poland, 18th century. Gift of Dr. Harry G. Friedman, The Jewish Museum, New York.

Al HaNissim — "For the Miracles," the Ḥanukkah prayer recited as part of the *Amidah* and *Birkat HaMazon* on the eight days.

Antiochus Epiphanes — The name of King Antiochus IV of Syria.

Apocrypha — The semi-holy collection of books in which the *Books of the Maccabees* are found.

Dreidel — A special four-sided top; a favorite Ḥanukkah game.

Hallel — Prayers of praise *(Psalms 113-118)*

Ḥanukkah Gelt — Gifts of coins to the children (and to charity).

Ḥanukkah — The post-biblical holiday commemorating the victory of the Maccabees over the Syrian Greeks in 165 B.C.E.

Ḥanukkiah — The Hebrew word for the eight-branched Ḥanukkah candlestick *(m'norah)*.

Hasmonean — Pertaining to the family name of the Maccabees.

Hellenism — An effort to emulate and imitate the Greek culture.

Kislev — The third month of the Hebrew (lunar) calendar.

Latke — Ḥanukkah pancake (Yiddish).

L'vivot — Pancakes.

Maccabee — "The Hammer"; the adopted name which Judah, the Hasmonean, added to his own.

Maccabiah — Athletic contests, associated with Ḥanukkah in Israel.

Maoz Tzur — "Rock of Ages"; traditionally sung by Ashkenazim after the kindling of the ḥanukkiah.

Mattathias — Hasmonean Priest who led Jews to route the armies of Antiochus Epiphanes.

M'norah — (Also · Menorah) The seven branched candelabrum found in the Temple and in every synagogue; the Ḥanukkah candelabrum is often called by this name, although its proper designation is *ḥanukkiah.*

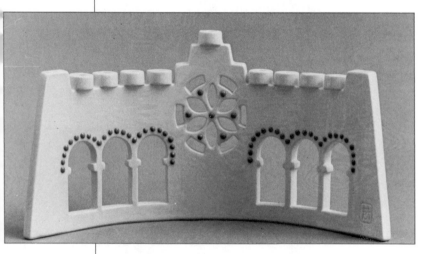

Modi'in — The town where the Hasmonean family lived when the revolt began.

Ner — Candle.

Nes — Miracle; banner.

Rosette Window M'norah by Arnold Schwarzbart, clay, 1981, Knoxville, Tennessee.

Psalm 30 — Recited daily during the eight days of the festival: *"Mizmor Shir Ḥanukkat HaBa'yit"* — "A psalm, a song for Ḥanukkah."

Shamash — ("Servant") The candle used to kindle the Ḥanukkah lights.

Sufganiyot — Jelly doughnuts, eaten in Israel during Ḥanukkah.

Sukkot — Festival of Tabernacles.

S'vivon — Dreidel.

Tz'dakah — Just and proper action; frequently translated as "charity".

Urim — Lights.

Ḥanukkah M'norah silver and brass, Warsaw, 19th century. Temple Israel of Great Neck, New York.

NOTES

NOTES

NOTES

NOTES

NOTES

NOTES

NOTES

NOTES

NOTES

NOTES